easy origami

EASY MAGICIAN
Origami

by Christopher L. Harbo

CAPSTONE PRESS
a capstone imprint

First Facts is published by Capstone Press,
1710 Roe Crest Drive, North Mankato, Minnesota 56003.
www.capstonepub.com

Books published by Capstone Press are manufactured with paper
containing at least 10 percent post-consumer waste.

Library of Congress Cataloging-in-Publication Data
Harbo, Christopher L.
  Easy magician origami / by Christopher L. Harbo.
     p. cm.—(First facts. Easy origami)
  Includes bibliographical references.
  ISBN 978-1-4296-6000-6 (library binding)
  1. Origami—Juvenile literature. 2. Magic tricks—Juvenile literature. 3. Magic tricks in art—Juvenile
literature. I. Title. II. Series.
  TT870.H32155 2012
  736'.982—dc22
                                                                            2011001010

Summary: Provides instructions and photo-illustrated diagrams for making a variety of easy,
magic-related origami models.

Editorial Credits
Designer: GENE BENTDAHL
Photo Studio Specialist: SARAH SCHUETTE
Scheduler: MARCY MORIN
Production Specialist: LAURA MANTHE

Photo Credits
Capstone Studio/Karon Dubke, all photos

Artistic Effects
Nova Development Corporation

ABOUT THE AUTHOR

Christopher L. Harbo loves origami. He began folding paper several years ago and hasn't quit since. In addition to decorative origami, he also enjoys folding paper airplanes. When he's not practicing origami, Christopher spends his free time reading Japanese comic books and watching movies.

Printed in the United States of America in North Mankato, Minnesota.
112012   006976R

TABLE OF Contents

PAPER MAGIC

Get ready to cast a magic spell on paper. This book is bursting with seven simple models that have to do with magic. Fold a pointy wizard's hat you can wear. Make a magic wand you can wave. Turn a dollar bill into a bow tie. Your friends and family will be amazed by your creations. Wiggle your fingers, and start making some paper magic!

MATERIALS

Origami is a simple art that doesn't use many materials. You'll only need the following things to complete the projects in this book:

Origami Paper: Square origami paper comes in many fun colors and sizes. You can buy this paper in most craft stores.

Ruler: Some models use measurements to complete. A ruler will help you measure.

Scissors: Sometimes a model needs a snip here or there to complete. Keep a scissors nearby.

Pencil: Use a pencil when you need to mark spots you measure with the ruler.

Craft Supplies: Markers and other craft supplies will help you decorate your models.

FOLDING TECHNIQUES

Folding paper is easier when you understand basic origami folds and symbols. Practice the folds on this list before trying the models in this book. Turn back to this list if you get stuck on a tricky step, or ask an adult for help.

Valley Folds are represented by a dashed line. One side of the paper is folded against the other like a book. A sharp fold is made by running your finger along the fold line.

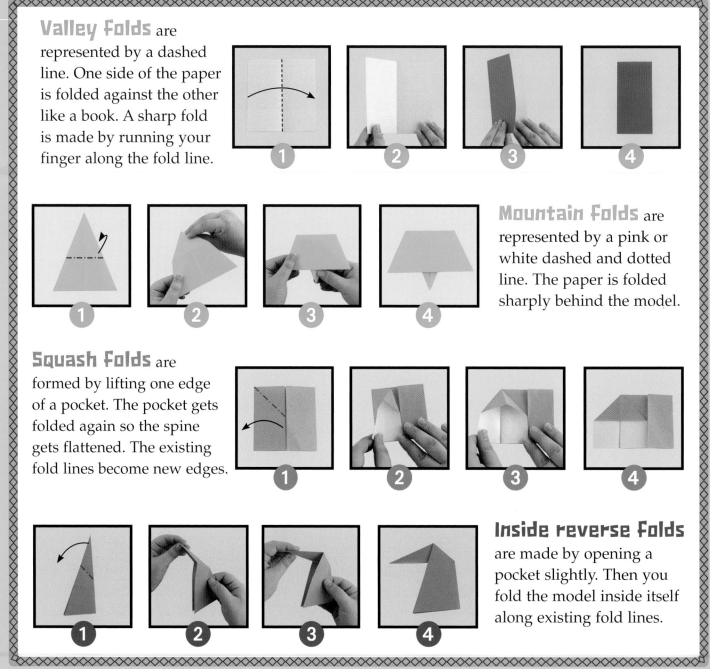

Mountain Folds are represented by a pink or white dashed and dotted line. The paper is folded sharply behind the model.

Squash Folds are formed by lifting one edge of a pocket. The pocket gets folded again so the spine gets flattened. The existing fold lines become new edges.

Inside reverse folds are made by opening a pocket slightly. Then you fold the model inside itself along existing fold lines.

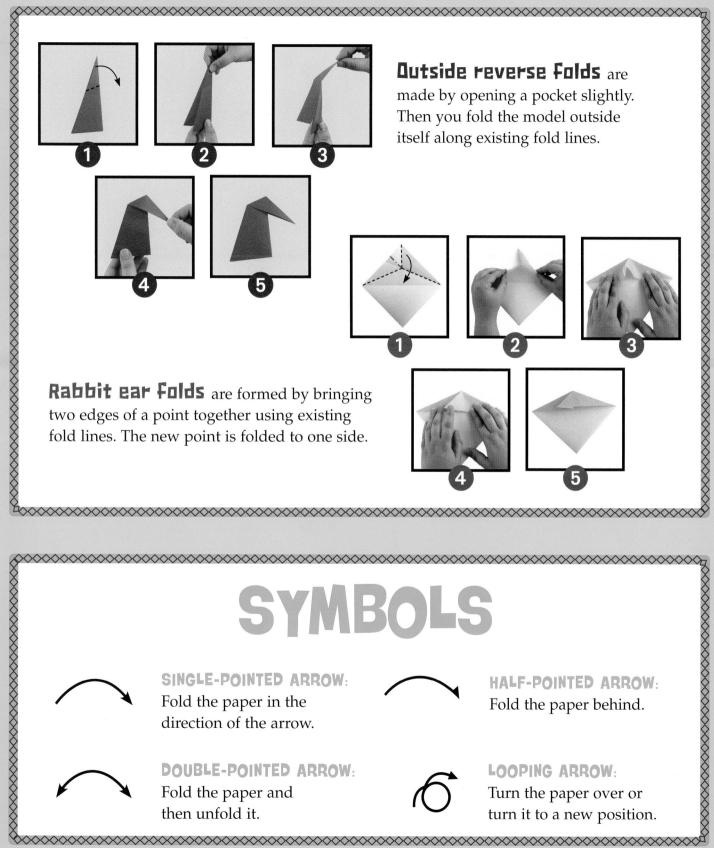

Outside reverse folds are made by opening a pocket slightly. Then you fold the model outside itself along existing fold lines.

Rabbit ear folds are formed by bringing two edges of a point together using existing fold lines. The new point is folded to one side.

SYMBOLS

SINGLE-POINTED ARROW:
Fold the paper in the direction of the arrow.

DOUBLE-POINTED ARROW:
Fold the paper and then unfold it.

HALF-POINTED ARROW:
Fold the paper behind.

LOOPING ARROW:
Turn the paper over or turn it to a new position.

LUCKY Rabbit

Traditional Model

Every magician has a lucky rabbit. You'll make this paper rabbit appear in seven simple steps.

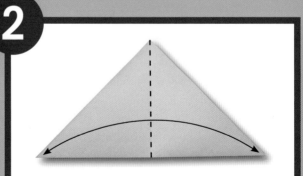

1 Start with the colored side of the paper face down. Valley fold the bottom point to the top point.

2 Valley fold the left point to the right point and unfold.

3 Valley fold the bottom edge. Make this fold about 1 inch (2.5 centimeters) above the bottom edge.

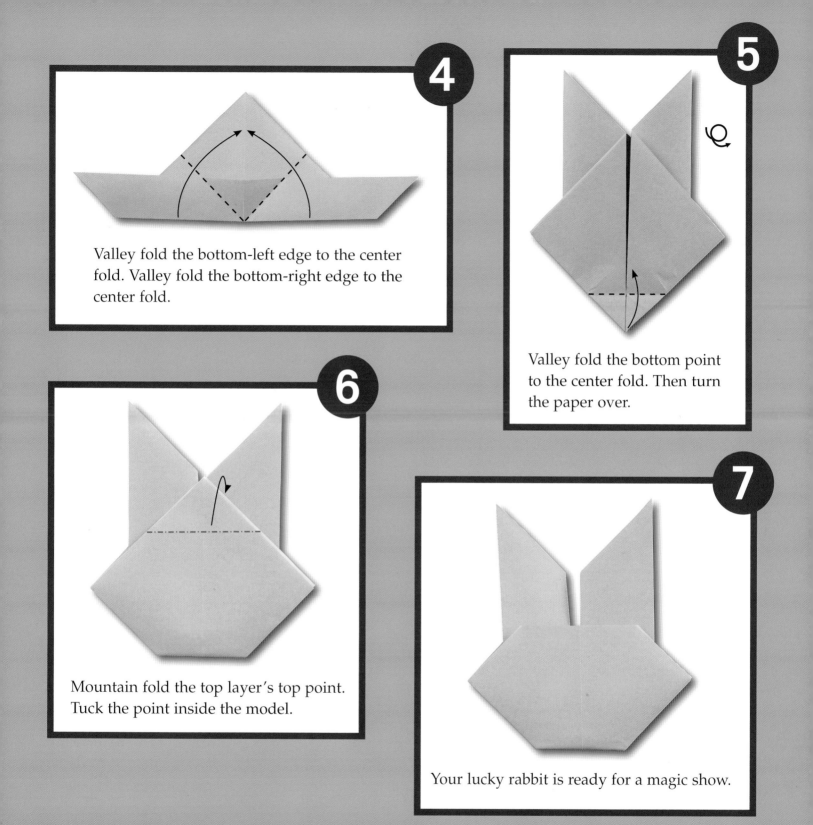

4

Valley fold the bottom-left edge to the center fold. Valley fold the bottom-right edge to the center fold.

5

Valley fold the bottom point to the center fold. Then turn the paper over.

6

Mountain fold the top layer's top point. Tuck the point inside the model.

7

Your lucky rabbit is ready for a magic show.

SECRET Tip Give your rabbit a fun face with googly eyes and yarn whiskers.

WIZARD'S Hat

Traditional Model

Turn yourself into a wizard with a magic hat made of paper. Put it on to cast your spells in style.

1

Begin with the colored side of the paper face down. Valley fold the top point to the bottom point.

2

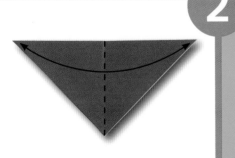

Valley fold the left point to the right point and unfold.

3

Use a ruler and a pencil to mark the bottom-left edge of the model. The mark should be 2 inches (5 cm) from the bottom point.

4

Valley fold the top-right edge to the mark made in step 3. Note how the fold begins at the center fold.

5

Valley fold the top-left edge even with the slanted edge made in step 4.

6

Grab the bottom point of the top layer. Valley fold this point up as far as it will go.

7

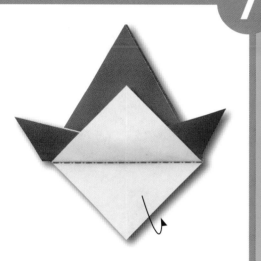

Mountain fold the bottom point behind the model.

8

Pull the top and bottom layers of the model apart to open the hat.

9

Cast a spell in your wizard's hat.

SECRET Tip To wear the wizard's hat, fold it with an 18-inch (46-cm) square of newspaper.

MAGIC Wand

Designed by Christopher L. Harbo

A magician never leaves home without a magic wand. But if you do, this paper wand is easy to fold in a pinch.

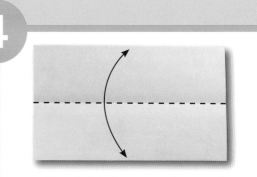

1

Use a scissors to cut a square piece of paper in half.

2

Begin with one of the halves colored side face up. Valley fold the left edge to the right. Make this fold about 1.5 inches (3.8 cm) from the left edge.

3

Turn the paper over.

4

Valley fold the top edge to the bottom edge and unfold.

5

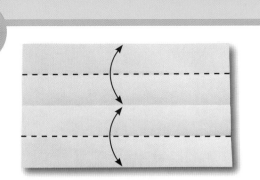

Valley fold the top edge to the center fold and unfold. Valley fold the bottom edge to the center fold and unfold.

6

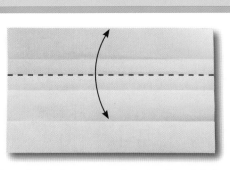

Valley fold the top edge to the fold between the center fold and the bottom edge. Make a firm fold and then unfold.

7

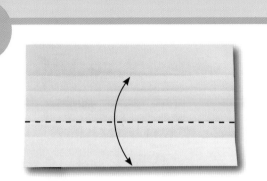

Valley fold the bottom edge to the second fold above the center fold. Make a firm fold and unfold.

8

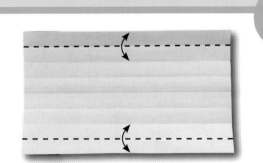

Valley fold the top edge to its nearest fold and unfold. Valley fold the bottom edge to its nearest fold and unfold.

9

Bring the top edge and bottom edge together.

10

Tuck the first two sections of the top edge into the bottom edge's flap. The paper will form a long tube.

11

Abracadabra! Your wand is ready to wave.

SECRET Tip Your paper wand is hollow. Stuff it with a handkerchief. Then pretend to magically pull it out of the end of your wand.

TOP Hat

Designed by Christopher L. Harbo

Your magic act isn't complete without a top hat.
Surprise your friends by pulling an origami
model out of the hat's secret pocket.

1

Begin with the colored
side of the paper face
down. Valley fold the
top edge to the bottom
edge and unfold.

2

Valley fold the top
edge to the center
fold. Valley fold
the bottom edge
to the center fold.

3

Valley fold the left edge to
the right edge and unfold.

4

Valley fold the left edge to
the center fold and unfold.

5

Valley fold the top-left corner to
the fold made in step 4. Make a
firm fold and unfold. Repeat this
step on the bottom-left corner.

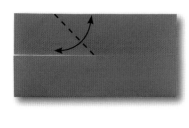

6

Valley fold the top-right edge to the fold made in step 4. Make the fold down to the center fold and unfold.

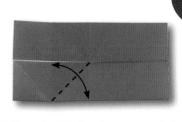

7

Valley fold the bottom-right edge to the fold made in step 4. Make the fold up to the center fold and unfold.

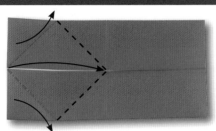

8

Squash fold the left side of the paper on the existing folds. This fold allows the left side's inside corners to swing above and below the edges of the model.

9

Valley fold the left edge to the center fold.

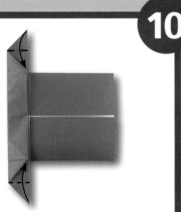

10

Valley fold the top point along the slanting edge. Valley fold the bottom point along the slanting edge.

11

Turn the model over.

12

You're ready to pull a paper rabbit out of your top hat!

SECRET Tip Open the top of the hat to find the secret pocket. Stuff it with the rabbit or dove models in this book.

LOVELY DOVE

Traditional Model

The lovely dove is light and thin. It's the perfect model to hide up your sleeve.

1 Start with the colored side of the paper face down. Valley fold the top corner to the bottom corner and unfold.

2 Valley fold the left corner to the right corner.

3 Valley fold the right corner's top layer to the left. Make the fold about 1.5 inches (3.8 cm) from the left edge.

4 Valley fold the top point to the bottom point.

5 Valley fold the top wing. Note how the fold is made where the slanted edge ends. Repeat this step on the back wing.

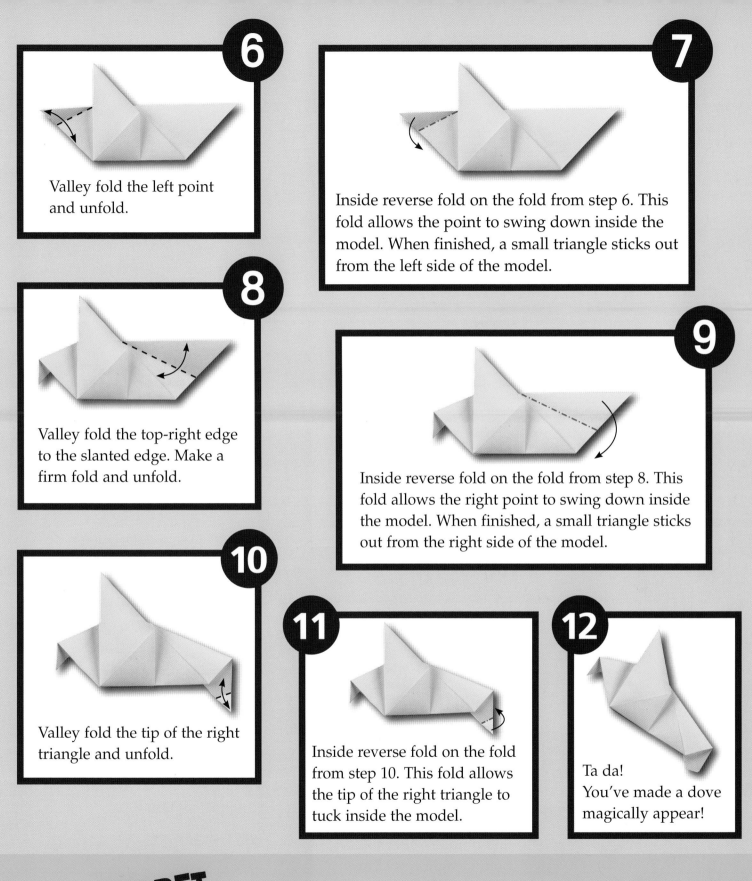

6 Valley fold the left point and unfold.

7 Inside reverse fold on the fold from step 6. This fold allows the point to swing down inside the model. When finished, a small triangle sticks out from the left side of the model.

8 Valley fold the top-right edge to the slanted edge. Make a firm fold and unfold.

9 Inside reverse fold on the fold from step 8. This fold allows the right point to swing down inside the model. When finished, a small triangle sticks out from the right side of the model.

10 Valley fold the tip of the right triangle and unfold.

11 Inside reverse fold on the fold from step 10. This fold allows the tip of the right triangle to tuck inside the model.

12 Ta da! You've made a dove magically appear!

SECRET Tip Curl the wings of the dove downward to give it a more lifelike look.

17

MONEY Bow Tie

Traditional Model

Why spend money when you can wear it? Dress up your magician's costume with a money bow tie.

1

Start with the president's side of the dollar face down. Valley fold the top edge to the bottom edge and unfold.

2

Valley fold the top-left corner to the center fold. Repeat this step with the other three corners.

3

Valley fold the top edge to the center fold. Valley fold the bottom edge to the center fold.

4

Valley fold the right point to the left point.

5

Valley fold the top-right corner to the center fold and unfold. Valley fold the bottom-right corner to the center fold and unfold.

6

Inside reverse fold the top-right corner on the folds made in step 5. This fold will allow the corner to tuck inside the model. Repeat this step with the bottom-right corner.

7

Valley fold the right point to the center fold.

8

Grab the back layer of the model, and swing it to the front.

10

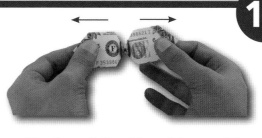

Open the model by pulling the top layer to the right.

9

Grab the right corners of the top layer. Valley fold these corners to the center fold. Repeat this step on corners of the back layer.

11

Gently pull the sides of the model apart to flatten the center knot.

12

Presto! You've turned a dollar bill into a bow tie.

SECRET Tip Make bow ties in any color or pattern you like. Just cut your paper to the same size as a dollar bill.

FORTUNE-Teller

Traditional Model

You don't need special powers to see into the future. Fold an origami fortune-teller to find out what the future holds.

1

Start with the colored side of the paper face down. Valley fold the top edge to the bottom edge and unfold. Valley fold the left edge to the right edge and unfold.

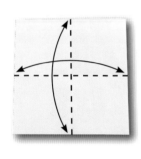

2

Valley fold all four corners to the center fold.

3

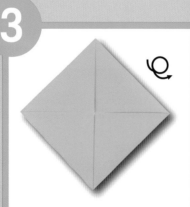

Turn the paper over.

4

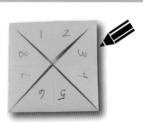

Valley fold all four corners to the center fold.

5

Use a pencil to write different numbers on each of the eight small triangles.

6

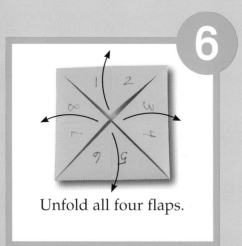

Unfold all four flaps.

7

Write fortunes on each of the flap's triangles. Then refold all four flaps, and turn the model over.

8

Write different colors on each of the four squares. When finished, turn the model over.

9

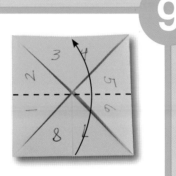

Valley fold the bottom edge to the top edge.

10

Slide your thumbs and index fingers into each of the four bottom pockets.

11

Push up and to the center until the points meet and the pockets open.

12

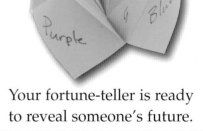

Your fortune-teller is ready to reveal someone's future.

PLAY Hint Have a friend pick a color. Open and close the fortune-teller once for every letter of that color. Have your friend pick a number. Lift the flap to see your friend's fortune.

21

READ More

Boursin, Didier. *Folding for Fun.* Richmond Hill, Ont.: Firefly Books, 2007.

Engel, Peter. *10-Fold Origami: Fabulous Paperfolds You Can Make in 10 Steps or Less.* New York: Sterling Pub. Co., Inc., 2008.

Harbo, Christopher L. *Easy Animal Origami.* Easy Origami. Mankato, Minn.: Capstone Press, 2011.

Meinking, Mary. *Easy Origami.* Origami. Mankato, Minn.: Capstone Press, 2009.

INTERNET Sites

FactHound offers a safe, fun way to find Internet sites related to this book. All of the sites on FactHound have been researched by our staff.

Here's all you do:

Visit *www.facthound.com*
Type in this code: 9781429660006

Super-cool stuff! Check out projects, games and lots more at
www.capstonekids.com